KINDERGO

Creating Magical Reading Moments

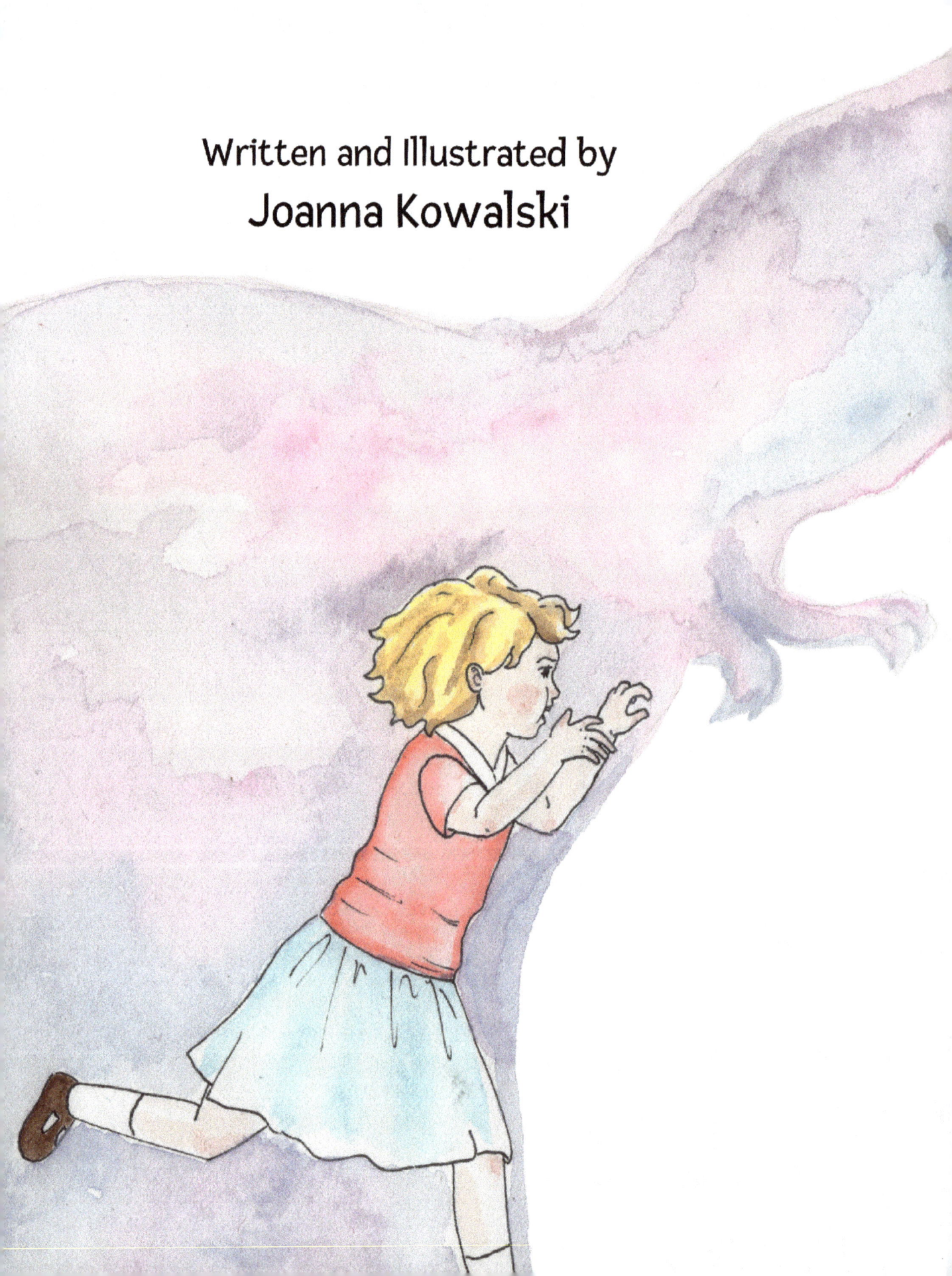

Written and Illustrated by
Joanna Kowalski

I WANT TO BE A DINOSAUR

I want to be a dinosaur
'Cause dinosaurs are cool.
They don't have any homework,
Or even go to school.

I wouldn't have to clean my room
Or do any of my chores,
I wouldn't need to have a bath,
That's not for dinosaurs!

I'd roam and play outside all day
And I'd be wild and free;

The trouble is I don't quite know which dinosaur I'd be!

Perhaps a stegosaurus,
With stout legs and a tough back;
I'd be strong enough to give
Our Baby Kate a piggy back.

Maybe a brachiosaurus
Is what I'd like to be.
I could save the neighbour's cat
If she got stuck in a tree.

I'd **ROOOOOAAAAARR!**
And chase them all away.

Or maybe a velociraptor;
I could run so fast!
Everyone would cheer me on
As I went racing past.

If I were a triceratops,
With a funny frilly head,
I'd visit friends, and make them laugh
If they were sick in bed.

If I were a dinosaur,
I think I'd miss some things;

Like visiting my friend Ruthie,
And playing on the swings.

I'd miss my teacher, Mrs James and all of Kindy B.

If I were a dinosaur They'd be too small for me!

I'd miss snuggling with Baby Kate
And baking with my mother.

I'd be too big to climb the trees
And play with my big brothers.

I couldn't hold a pen or paint,
Or draw, or sing, or write.
I'd miss all Daddy's stories,
And Mum kissing me goodnight.

I'd like to be a dinosaur;
I love them all, you see.
But being a girl is pretty good;
I'd like to just be me.

The End

www.ingramcontent.com/pod-product-compliance
Lightning Source LLC
LaVergne TN
LVHW070949070426
835507LV00029B/3464